THE WAY DOWN

PRINCETON SERIES OF CONTEMPORARY POETS

For other books in the series, see page 77.

The Way Down

By John Burt

PRINCETON UNIVERSITY PRESS

Published by Princeton University Press, 41 William Street,
Princeton, New Jersey 08540
In the United Kingdom: Princeton University Press,
Guildford, Surrey

Library of Congress Cataloging in Publication Data will be
found on the last printed page of this book

ISBN 0-691-06727-9 (cloth)
          01443-4 (pbk.)

Publication of this book has been aided by the
Whitney Darrow Fund of Princeton University Press

This book has been composed in Linotron Sabon

Printed in the United States of America
by Princeton University Press
Princeton, New Jersey

Acknowledgments

"Plains of Peace" and "Teratocarcinoma" appeared in *The Yale Review*.

"Winter: Hunters in Snow" appeared in *Webster Review*.

"Three Songs from Paintings by J. E. Millais" and "The Zeppelin Watchers" appeared in *Poetry Miscellany*.

"After the Thunderstorm" appeared in *The Spirit that Moves Us*.

"Robert Falcon Scott Enters Paradise" appeared in *Chicago Review*.

"Ariadne," "From the Diary of Willard Gibbs," "Photograph from Luzon, 1899," "Songs of Innocence," and "Trucks on a Hill in Winter" appeared in *Cumberland Poetry Review*.

"St. Francis and the Wolf," "Waiting for Birds," "Andrew Ramsay at the Somme," and "Paolo and Francesca" appeared in *Shenandoah*.

I would like to thank the Ingram Merrill Foundation for its generous support.

For Donna, with love

CONTENTS

THE TRIUMPH OF LOVE

The Funeral Day

(Suffield, Connecticut, 1952)

Later, we folded our hands in his tidy room.
Patience taught us nothing: we sat for hours
While the brass clock mumbled to itself like a nun.
The shadows in the eaves began
To knot up all the air. And then outside
This bird just sang and sang and sang.
What was it to him? Where did he get the right?
I got up to close the window

And there I saw the tobacco-fields
Moving their shrouds in the dusk.
The wind came thoughtlessly over the wide cloth
And lifted the white undersides of leaves.
I didn't close the window. When I sat back down,
I didn't say what I had seen.

Three Songs from Paintings
by J. E. Millais

I. THE BLIND GIRL

The thrush was quiet, and the buzz of insects
Ceased to stumble in my ear. I said:
Sister, it is about to rain.
But she tugged my hand
And led me through the cool of day.
In the rattle of the leaves, the distant thunder
Hid its breath. Is there a tree,
I said, to shelter us awhile?
She pulled me on and did not say a word.

But you will be afraid, I thought,
When the storm comes striding on the plain;
And we will cower by the highway's side,
And you will cling to me, amid the shattered air
As if I were your dream.
I will hear the storm departing
Long before it ends for you,
And my heart will leap to meet the rainbow
You will only see.

II. The Bridesmaid

As you look at nothing, turning a ring in your hand,
Your lips part.
What reflection surfaces behind your eyes?
For half an hour you are silent
In the eddies of your hair.

If the perfume, and the smell of oranges
Were to unfold, if the sullen moon
Were to crease the coverts, as once it did
When wind went heaving through the dark—

You start. The candle on the table sways.
Somewhere a diver claws the soundless water
And then is still.
Quietly inhaling, you touch the flowers at your breast
And rise as slowly from the mirror as a star.

III. Mariana in the Moated Grange

Long shadows glide to the ground.
Among plane trees, the wind moves
Like the memory of wind.
Yellow leaves, shifting on the windowsill,
Fall like light.
The poison flower painted on the glass
Is a bending angel, an angel in disgrace.
In the recesses of the room,
Among September's purple disarray,
An unseen candle burns.

But it is no vision that moves among the leaves
Scattered on the floor, no dream that slants
Across the casement like the shadow of a man.

By the windowsill, where the sun of afternoon
Condensed upon the air, she had been weaving,
Singing to herself a song ten summers old.
But when the words ran out
And the dust bloomed in the light, she stood
And stretched amid the quiet of the room
Her eyes as empty as the wind.

Songs of Innocence

(Newport, 1886)

It is not narcissism, nor vanity,
But the blithe and gaudy irony of play
That paints the mouth a burning bud, arches
Tense the bow on brow, and sets the hectic
Spot on laughing cheek. Look mommy!
She cries, until she does.

                  Drawing breath,
She smiles hastily, discovering there
Not herself undone in wicked blazon,
Not the portent of hunger, sign of sorrow
Declared but not imagined, inevitable
But not realized. It is young bravery
Repeating the brave things she only later
Learns to mean, sure to stray, but sure
In straying, bound for shade, yet stopping here
To play with shades she later will assume.

Ballet Academy

It suits him fine to loiter in the late
Slant of winter light: the blind buildings
Keep their distance, and the air's austerity
Pleases him, and teaches him not to want.
It is not the weather that betrays.

Lesson's over: the girls' voices wake him,
And the glass door opens noiselessly. The room
Is warm, too warm, he tells himself, looking
At his feet. The linoleum is pink.
And so also the walls: pink cinder-block.
Their voices flutter in their inner room
Where they have been reaching, turning, bending,
In fierce red light streaming from high slats
Through dense shadows, tropical. "And you are?"
Startled, he tells her. She stands there smiling.
"A darling girl," she says, "She'll be right out."
She looks at him, smiling a bit too long,
Setting an old ache loose. But the girl comes,
Taking his hand, clearing the air with talk,
And leads him back into the cold, at last.

Ariadne

The water burns on the sand. Here
Is an arch. There a pillar.
Everywhere the sun.

In my father's house there are so many rooms
That I have lost myself for hours at a time.
Unspeaking slaves with jars of oil
Drown my footsteps in their own.
From every light well the same
Uncomprehending blue eye looks down. So
I have come to the edge of the sea.

Black sail, black keel, black wave,
What man is brother to me? Will he
Become a thing of corridors?
Will he become as shameful in his sight
As I am in my own?

Let this be a city which never knew a king,
A city without statues,
Built by no hand.
If a name is on the wall,
A guilty child scratched it there.
And let those who cross the ocean
Find among its avenues
No casks of wine, Phoenician gold,
Or shadows to be buried in.

The ocean's blue is the blue of the sky.
The sound of waves collapsing on the harbor bar
Cannot be parted from the wind.

The marble arches wither in the sun.

Paolo and Francesca

It only seemed a tempest. On the warm
Whirling of the wind we slid, and gave
Ourselves into its fullness. Sweet and grave,
The sorrow of her face composed the storm
Till we forgot our fear, and beating higher,
Our hearts grew keen and awful as the sun.
Dreams wound us in, and we became as one
Who looks into the mirror of desire.

Her mouth was clay, and on my lips the chill
Stole inward with a less than mortal sting
Whose promise and enthrallment were the same.
O you, who make a kingdom of the will,
In angel hunger for a human thing,
Your recompense is having what you claim.

Waiting for Birds

It wasn't half so strange to wake alone
As she had feared, she told herself, awake,
Waiting for birds, when night had cleared for her.
How proud of her he'd be, to see her now,
Who learned her bravery by heart from him.
The air was still as sorrow, and as cool.
If death were like this hour, yes, if death
Were breathing in the purple dark and calm,
Why then, it must be lucky and delicious,
And easy, easy and rich to let it take.
Is this the way? She lay so still, so ready,
She felt the little plates in every vein
Turn into gems. The nerves, unknotted, rayed
Their silver wire. And all of her was perfect,
All forgotten. This is how they lay
Forever in the sure repose of loss:
Outside, the stone sarcophagus, the charms
Against all suffering, against all hope;
Then ritual gold and lapis lazuli,
The body wrought by grief beyond decay;
Then, wrapped in linen, fragrant herbs, and balm,
A few charred random flakes of flesh.
But all at once an urgency of birds
Broke in her ear, glass ground on glass
Till up she leapt, raging and revived.
Birds, what can she tell you but never to rest?
Who doesn't eat his heart must let it rot.

On the Will to Believe

Who is awake? The wind is awake.
But will you stir? Her wakefulness is part of yours.
Will you walk with her in the darkness?
Here is the star she stole for you alone.
She will show to you a tree of thorns,
Her empty hands, that broken bridge.
You will read in the book of faces
But you will not find your own.

And you will remember then to stop, to lie
Down still, to say that if there were a mark
It would be there, and there would demonstrate
The love, the will, the calm necessity.
The clouds will scud among the glaciers of the mountain.
The idiot moon will watch in the cold.

Learning the Table

What we cannot grasp
We get by heart,
Repeating our
Misgiving's part

Until it's ours
If any is:
Our hot, unmeaning
Parodies

That seem and seem
But cannot be
Till they rehearse
Our liberty

And master us
And make us new.
Then we desire
What we must do

And choose again
Misgiving's part:
What we cannot grasp
We get by heart.

Teratocarcinoma

I know thee not, nor ever saw
Sight more detestable than him or thee.

Paradise Lost

From the Greek *teras*, monster:
A heterogeneous tumor.
Immortal and confused,
It walks the twisted stair of self,
An embryo god, pluripotent,
Looking for what will last.
Here is a shard of bone.
Was it mine in eternity?
It shall be mine again.
Where there should be marrow it places hair.
This tangled net of nerve, is it also mine?
What I recognize I shall retain.
Nothing will be lost to me.
It folds a tooth in the midst of its flesh.
I shall not die. Sinew, cartilage, and seed
I use, but am not bound by them.
I have descended out of order and mortality.
Forever it will wonder at itself,
A lonely solipsist, lost in the genes,
Heaping shape on shape, untiring,
Trying to remember where it first went wrong,
Forgetting that death is not the price of sin
But mercy's tender innovation.

The Homecoming of Bran

So we bore the body of Bran beyond the gates
And placed him at the table's head.
We drank with him, and he did not decay.
We slept in shadows, and he did not close his eyes.
And for twenty months we heard the songs
Which the birds of Rhiannon sing for the weary and the dead.
And we saw no man other than ourselves.
And we poured our laughter on the ground.
And the sun laughed in his strength
Until Heilyn said,
"Where are the fields of this country?"
And we opened the east gate
And found nor fields nor pastures
Nor any cultivated land.
And Heilyn said,
"Where are the towns of this country?"
We opened the south gate
And found nor house nor hut
Nor wall of any kind.
And Heilyn said,
"Where are the men of this country?"
We opened the north gate
And saw the speechless shape
Of a man in fur, climbing the rocks far away.
And then we opened the west gate

And all our lands were there, and we remembered
Every blow we took beyond the sea,
And remembered our wives, that wailed us as widows,
And remembered the death of Prince Bran:
Whose body we burnt to ashes.
When we returned to our halls,
Strange men sat on all our thrones.

King Mark's Dream

It was the fumes of wine, that's all,
And sleeping all alone in that big hot bed.
He stood awhile at the sill: the stubble-rows
Were muffled up in snow. An empty tree shook,
And from the forest came the cries of distant wolves.
It was a dream. She was not flesh and blood.
And I am old to be so hot. I will pray
For an easy death before I lose myself.

But it was not death he woke to, not death
Who sat beside him, stilled his heart,
And loosened all the knots that held his breath,
But the child he found weeping at his door,
Who over again would count the names of woe,
Whom he had christened "love" and taught to whisper "mine."

From the Diary of
Willard Gibbs

(March, 1903)

I wanted to write about "The Mind and Nature,"
One abstraction searching out another.
But the mind is never just itself.
We love Theory as poets love pale women,
For its perfection and its lack of pity.
And our love is just as happy.
Who can say which killed Galois:
The dancing girl for whose sake
He had his brains blown out in a duel;
Or her, less sensuous but no less coy,
His Theory, its freedom and pure promise,
What he fought his teachers for,
Wrote theorems out that no one read
(Or read as his calm mistress
Read his verses), until he lived apart
And sought unhappy company?
He saw too much perfection, and it unmanned him.
His letter to Gauss, that last night, is that
The Mind alone with Nature?
—Tear-stained and garbled, thick with his fear,
But willing his one clarity
To one he scarce believed would read it through?

Enough: I have myself preferred to compromise,
To teach mechanics to backward children
My treatise on gears, they said, had more geometry

Than iron in it, and the engine-governor
I built showed some new things about control.
I taught my classes and was free of them.

But in a cold house, on quiet nights
I traced my limits clearly as I could,
And found in them a Theory of my own.
I learned that every order runs to rot,
That every motion must in time be spent.
There must be loveliness in that unlovely law.

I gave it homage; I could not give it love.
I have, at least, survived my theories,
But did I master them by knowing them,
Or have I just lived too long?

The mind, I know. Nature casts me out.

Photograph from Luzon, 1899

He is fifteen in the picture, fighting in the Philippines,
Wearing a medic's uniform too large for him.
Some naked children, forgetting their game,
Look up at him but do not speak.
In a second they will run away,
And he, not seeing them, will still be standing straight,
Hands on hips, like one disdaining trial.

He did not have it taken for his parents—who were they?—
Nor for the aunt who, knowing, pitying,
Forgave him till she justified his contempt.
He had it taken for history's sake, having none,
His taunt to those who knew but would not tell
The unremembered grievance he fostered like a twin.

Those he bandaged, who cried out
Jesus when he pulled the dressings tight,
Saw that it was not the enemy alone he hated.
His captain said it was the strain of war,
Of fighting an enemy who crept
Between the pickets in the dark
And set the tents afire.

Was it the not knowing, or what he did not know?

The night before, a Filipino woman
Had surprised him, had touched his arm
In mute offer and entreaty. Later,
Having beaten her till she ran, he dreamed
Of women, pale and long-haired women
Who took him in their arms, saying
Sleep, sleep, it is enough,
And woke up reaching, wondering.

And then, lost in an unmastered past,
He fixed time's center *here*, glaring
At the glib photographer whose name he never learned,
Saying to himself, *Hold on to this,*
You who search my giddiness and pain.
This is what I was.
See now if you can master me.

His Kind-Hearted Woman

When Robert Johnson sang alone in hell
A tree sprang up, its branches phosphorescent
In the still gloom, its gleaming bark all silver
And all its leaves transparent, amethyst.
He touched a limb, and leaf on leaf onsliding
Shook out the timid sound of wakened bells.
He found in every secrecy of leaves
A fruit: he watched it rolling in his palm
Then put it cautiously into his mouth,
Its taste electric, bitter, passing quickly
Into nothing. At last they stained his hands,
As he was pulling from that ringing tree
Again and again, and the glittering storm of leaves
Shook over him their wakeful quavering.

And men and women came to him in hell
Awakened by the tree he'd set to cry,
Each eye insistent, each tongue full of blame,
Its candor loud and horrible and right,
How they'd been wronged, how they were not the first
To lose their way in love, how strange it was.
But every heart a hard uncertainty
Clutched tightly to itself as if in hope
That they might yet be wrong, that love itself
Were more than tangling, though it tangled them,
That he might ravel out their love and rage.

They heard themselves, then stood there dumb, ashamed,
And saw they'd do again what they had done,
Who'd never love until they gave up hope.

She'd had a dream before she poisoned him:
While she lay sleeping, he stood at her door
And longing gripped her till she held her breath
And opened to him; but he wasn't there,
And she went walking in the night alone
Through barren streets and barren alleyways
All strange to her, inhuman, like no place,
And brutal strangers laid their hands on her
And tore her gown. She woke aghast and knew
How knowingly he'd wink, and drink it down,
As if it were as sweet to him as love,
How even in convulsions, on all fours,
Slipping in his blood, a beast enraged,
Still he would shout: I'm not afraid. I'm not.

Leonce Pontellier

I

He was so grateful they were nice to him
He almost put from sight the irony
They didn't know they felt, much less betrayed.
He didn't know what to allow himself.
That he had failed her he was well aware
Although he knew she'd never noticed it
Not having given him the chance to fail.
The words he might have used for what she'd done
"Deceit," "betrayal," "infidelity,"
Seemed grandiose and false. If that were grief
It ought to be a purer thing than what
He had these days been stalking in his mind,
Half doubting it was there, afraid at once
It might, or else might not, be stalking him.
He was her husband. He had a right to guilt,
To angry incredulity, to grief.
But what he felt was blank and at a loss.
He'd have to get his bearings from his friends,
Whose very kindness stopped him in his tracks.

He didn't doubt that they meant well by him,
For if he did, where would he find himself?
Not hell, for sure, he was already there,
Nor limbo, where he saw he'd been before.

Then paradise, for doubting them he'd hate,
And hating, burn to purity again.

He'd known, almost at once, how it would be:
They wouldn't fear to see themselves in him
(As he, God knows, would not have seen himself
Had it all happened to somebody else)
Because they thought him far too dull to blame.
They'd swaddle him in kindness like a child
Who mustn't learn what he can't bear to learn
And so learns nothing, except to crave and fear
That worst surmise he makes despite it all:
He'd never wronged her, for he'd never mattered.

But even Doctor Mandelet, who took
His elbow as he wobbled off the train
Into a crowd whose tongue had slipped his mind,
Parting the wave (How people put their hands
All over you in a crowd—are you unreal
To them?—as if that hidden little push
From nobody, that hot breath in the ear,
Were not more intimate than you can be
With anyone you love!), who had the only
Fully-formed intention in that stifling
Sweetness and love-languor of the air,

Was not so wise as to conceal his tact.

For heaven's sake, be careful, he kept thinking,
Maybe you are the only one in doubt.

When they were settled in the coach, he bent
His head to listen, waiting for his cue,
But the Doctor kept his counsel, as if he knew
Leonce's mind, but wouldn't show his own.

Nothing on the Gulf so cool as grief.
You never feel it when you lose an arm,
Although you feel it with you after that.
There was some other fellow suffering,
Happy not to be despised, and wishing
Not their love perhaps, but just some hint
Of how he ought to act.

      What they will know
Will be his six weeks skulking in New York.
"If he were certain that were cowardice,
The Doctor's charity would have more edge,
More conscious edge. So he must be in doubt
How much was fear or generosity.
He wants to do me justice; he's held back
The urge to pity and the urge to blame.
He sees me sitting in the lobbies, calm

But puzzled, hoping I've at least been wise,
Each day a bit persuaded, a bit more suave,
A bit more used to it, a bit less stung:
'Well! Edna will regain her wits and end
That dalliance—so unlike her!—she's begun
With—was it Robert LeBrun?—well, anyway
With someone silly and a little saccharine
Whom soon enough she'll find more dull than me
And will dismiss. At last she'll send to me
A charming note chock full of idleness
From which I'll know I can come South again
And notice nothing, forgiving in advance
What she can claim I never knew about
And so not be in debt to me at all.' "

The Doctor would be wrong here, that he knew,
And knew that all their friends would take his lead.
He had been terrified, but not of shame.
Let her sleep with any fool she might,
Under his very roof, upon his bed,
Let her wake their children with her cries,
Let her kiss him in the public street
Before his face—that would still be less
Than what he'd run from, what he saw in her,
That even she had not discovered there
But thought was Art or Liberty or Sex.
It was some other fear had made him run.

What they might think of her he didn't know.
"What if they hate her? Could that be possible?
Good God! Suppose they try to comfort me
By telling me what I don't want to know!

"They are not monsters; they will pity her.

"The Doctor is ashamed and reticent.
Poor Robert LeBrun, in South America,
Will think she did all this for love of him.
Poor boy, he even distanced me in flight
Though all he wanted was to save his name,
To keep himself from doing what—who knows?—
Might well have saved them both. Or him at least.
That is the Doctor's theory. It would be mine
If I were someone else, or she herself:
'Had Edna just been Creole, then she'd know
Just what to do with boredom, restlessness;
Your fun won't make the sun forget to rise.
But these Americans are always good
Until they're worse than they might need to be.'
He would not be ashamed of that. But is.
Which means there's something else, something beneath her,
Which he won't want to tell, but must forestall."

He knew they wouldn't let him see the body,
All bloated and discolored by the heat

And brine of two days dragging in the surf.
Think as he might all night the last few nights
He couldn't see her knee-deep in the warm
Insinuation of the ocean, its strength
Disguised as suavity, its gentleness
A kind of sensuous cruelty. Was her face
Rapt and transformed, as if that torrid pull
Was just the thing he was not master of,
A kind of manhood no man ever has
That only Leda fully understood?
Or was she calm, beyond that numbing force
She would not feel but be, a mortal riddle,
Severe, serene, completely without need,
Returning to the waves that gave her birth?
Would that be Edna, or some part of him?
He couldn't get it straight. He'd pinch himself
And there would be the Carolinas, blurred
In dark, the matron up the aisle asleep,
The pale light slanting down her open mouth.
The only Edna he could picture then
Would be too prickly and too ill at ease
To give herself to any wave. She'd catch
Herself about to strike a pose, and wince,
And wonder how she ever got in mind
Such fool romantic notions. That was it,
The thing he couldn't picture. He would see
Her face: mocking, sour, disappointed

In just that way that drove him wild but put
Her just beyond his reach, the face, that is,
Of someone who would never die for love,
Or any other thing she'd seen quite through.
And yet she had, apparently she had.

He saw a summer evening months ago.
How Edna had gone swimming just at dusk,
Who'd never even dipped her hand before,
Who'd thought the water rancid and unclean.
"Bravo! Bravo!" he'd shouted from the shore.
He had been pleased for her; it seemed so odd
That Edna, who'd outgallop any man
In New Orleans, should be afraid to swim.
(Even Madame LeClaire would hobble down
On aching feet to take a daily wade.)
She'd never swum alone, and yet her stroke
Was clean and swift and sleek, without a trace
Of that coy awkwardness that pulls men's hearts
With guilt and longing they mistake for love.
She swam just like a seal, her mastery
Not just mere expertise or strength, but candid
Certitude that she had seen it through,
Could find her way where there was not a way.
He caught his breath: At last she seemed at ease
Who'd had him worried all that summer long
With some vague peevishness he couldn't trace

But maybe she could trace, if how she swam
Were any sign. He should have trusted her
He told himself, when all at once she stopped
Dead in the water, looking out to sea,
Milling for a moment in the gold
Retreating shimmer of the even waves.
Leonce stood up to take a closer look
But couldn't see her for the setting sun.
He held his hands before him stupidly,
Then saw her swimming in, just as before.
At last, she stood knee deep in foam and wash,
Her back to him, watching night fall in,
Then turned and walked right past without a word.
As hours passed, she drifted to and fro,
The hammock gliding on the edge of shade,
One arm behind her head, her eyes unfixed:
He cleared his throat to ask ironically
Just when she planned on coming in to bed,
But felt abashed, and watched her swinging there,
Her mind on nothing he could understand.
He lit a panatela to pretend
He could outwait her with civility.
But drowsing in his chair he saw the dead
Beneath the water, peering through the murk,
Their hair grown long, their arms wrapped up in vines,
Their cheeks and eager lips full-flushed, awake,
Their white hands groping for the bayou's edge.

He woke to moth wings flittering in his face,
Went in alone, and lay there bolt awake
Listening to their children stir in sleep.

The carriage now was rolling steadily,
The streets more open, cooler, shaded here
By branches tentative, alive, shifting
Gingerly in a breeze nobody felt,
Fingering their faces, not knowing them.
"Leonce," the Doctor said, uncertainly,
As if unsure the even slap of hooves
Had stilled their minds enough for him to say
The unsaid thing he'd held so cautiously.
Leonce looked up then, eager, face alight.

But what he said was how they'd buried her
At once, the weather being hot: they hoped
He wouldn't think they meant to slight his rights.

He almost laughed before he caught himself.
Was that the cause of all the Doctor's tact?

"No, Doctor, you have done your best by me."
He smiled to put the older man at ease,
As if he were the comforter, his friend
A stumbling Job the slightest bit unsure

Not only that he had deserved it all,
But that some further thing were yet to lose.

"No, it only means he's lost his nerve
And what he's said will get him off the hook.
There must be something else he hasn't said.
He only knows what I know, though he has
Some fact he thinks explains it all, which makes
Him treat me cautiously lest I surprise
It out of him, and think what he believes
I cannot bear. It wasn't, then, for love,
For then he wouldn't be ashamed to say.
Unless she took someone so wrong, so false,
It leaves him wondering, without a clue.
But even that is not a clue at all,
Although he seems to think it one."

                              They stopped.
There was his house, half stripped of furniture,
The casements open like droop-lidded eyes.
He sat there pensive, at a loss, but when
The Doctor offered to conduct him in,
Not adding that he shouldn't be alone,
He shook his head. "I'll be all right," he said.

II

He knew at once it had been no mistake
To come out to the Island once again.
Five years he'd kept away, not scared of ghosts
But of propriety. Should Robert there,
His health long broken by malaria,
Catch sight of him, there would be awkwardness;
He would believe he'd come to show him up,
Or, even worse, to face the poor boy down
Not with his own resentment but that guilt
Leonce could guess he couldn't fully lose.
They met by chance down on Carondelet:
The boy was easing down the Doctor's steps
And had been recognized before he gained
The safety of the carriage waiting there.
Leonce did not hail-fellow him. He knew
That that, of all the false notes, would be worst.
He let himself be awkward, to put at ease
The young man's fear that he'd had some design.
He never had to let him off the hook:
That long incomprehension they had shared
Had made them more familiar than they'd known.
By lunch's end he'd been invited out
To see his mother at Grand Isle again
And also, this in unsaid gratitude

For not despising him, to lay to rest,
Perhaps, the unlaid ghost not of his wife,
But of his fear of her, his dim surmise
That he'd survived only by shallowness
What she had been too wise to see and live.

Madame LeBrun had wilted overnight,
Leonce perceived, as she was bantering him.
He'd heard from Robert she was ill, and saw
She bore herself as if an invalid
But didn't know, herself, just what was wrong,
And poured out gaiety by force of will
Not to deceive him, but to show herself
How foolish her misgivings all had been.
It was an effort just to look her age.
The place was Victor's now, but it was clear
His mother had no faith in him. At noon
The Spanish girl walked by, a basket full
Of dirty laundry in her arms. Madame
Excused herself, and rushed out of the room
Until the girl had passed. Her barefoot boy
Leonce could see at once was Victor's son
Down to the dirty face and spindly legs.
Leonce could hear the scene four years ago,
How Victor plausibly swore innocence,
Till she forgave what she had never quite
Accused him of, and tried with all her might

To take his word, until perhaps she did,
Or didn't care, or wouldn't ask herself.
There had been no one else but Victor left
To manage the hotel when she fell ill,
With Robert out of touch down in Cayenne
(Where he was bound the night that Edna died
To factor latex from the rubber farms
That thrived no better than his love or health).
She gave the place to him reluctantly.
And he had let it go, that much was clear.
The wicker chairs were musty and precarious,
The linen none too clean, the parrot dead.
The Creoles came no longer, still the rooms
Were full, with smaller businessmen from town,
Two families from Vicksburg, and—how strange!—
Old Mademoiselle Reisz, who nodded bitterly
As much to say she'd seen him, now keep off.
She noticed that the boys were not with him
And doubtless had her own ideas about
His purposes in coming to the Isle,
Not that it bothered her what he might do.
Leonce was stung. What did she think he was?
Madame LeBrun was nice, although her pert
Staccato bossiness, her busy chat,
Had faded into fussy discontent.
That he was Edna's husband she'd forgot;
—Of course, she knew exactly who he was,

But saw him as a link to better times
Come back without reflection or reproach.
They drank some Beaujolais she must have saved
From when they might have served such wine at whim
(Though like the place, it had seen better days)
And talked of nothing, but it was enough
To make her hide her avid hopelessness
And smile with that shy, half-conscious light
He might have flirted with had he been young,
And known she'd only take it as he meant.
He went with Robert later down to Klein's
And lost a bit at billiards as before.
All day he played it painfully by ear,
As they were doing, had done so beautifully
He almost thought they knew despite it all
How it would have to go, though if they did,
What need had they of him, what did he know
That made them heel so hard to courtesy?

They almost brought it off, the three of them,
He thought that night, in bed, not restlessly
(Not having faith enough for nervousness)
But stern and clear, as he had hoped to be
When lucid shame was new enough to seem
A kind of wisdom. It had been just as hard
As he'd expected, though he hadn't felt

That chilly panic and delirium
In which he knew, were he to lose himself,
It wouldn't matter if he found his way.
He hoped he hadn't come to ease his mind.
Though what he meant to do he wasn't sure.
Is shame a kind of mortgage that you pay
A little every year until it's gone?
And then what next? Tear up the bill? Be free?
Be just as stupid as you were before?
He hadn't come to settle anything,
Nor—Robert had been wrong—to lay his fear.
They were the only things he counted on
To keep him from an idiot reckoning.
His first idea was that he'd come to prove
To his misgivings just how far he'd come,
Except the need of proof itself made clear
How wishful his insistence was, how shrill.
He felt the pull of place, and came to find
What had attracted him, who knew full well
He couldn't know beforehand why he'd come,
Could never know till it was over with
Whether every motive had been base.
By then, of course, it would have been too late.
But not to know was worse. He knew at least
The things he hadn't come to find, the wishes
He'd had to learn to blunt. He might be safe.

At almost four the air was cool enough
To walk abroad. He dressed in fresher clothes
And sauntered down behind the summerhouse
To bayou-side. The moon was out, though hid
By fleshy leaves that dangled from the boughs
In dank and aimless imbecility
Groping for the water rich with rot.
It was like wandering in a human heart.
He knew the place, and there was nothing there.
He dropped a rock, to hear the sound of change,
Then heard a door behind him opening.
And Mademoiselle Reisz across the lawn
Peered from the dark veranda, fully dressed,
A ruby at her throat, her hands in gloves.
He held his breath till she went back inside.

Still shuddering at the falseness of his step,
He watched the windows harden, blue, opaque,
The columns gleaming in the wash of gray,
As if it held its breath, the quiet house.
It was a foolish guess. He was ashamed
But only now discovered why he'd dropped
The Doctor's theory that she'd shocked herself
By making love to Alcée Arobin
And wished for death before she lost her head
In more degrading ways with other men:

Like the Doctor, she also got it wrong
And had herself but dimly understood
What had been drawing her unerringly.

The beach was cool, and scattered, vagrant light
Lay nervous on the darkened water-paths.
She would be foreign there, had come by day
To wait there calmly in her element,
A huntress fierce in her virginity,
All sleek and white, her thrilling mockery
Turning eager followers to beasts.
It stirred and shamed him, beauty's cruelty.
But what would Beauty love, could Beauty love?

When nightfall came, she would be naked there,
Her body smooth and supple in the swell,
Her random hair in rich unrest, unbound.
When he arrived she would feel no surprise,
That coldest mariner of air, who knew
That she would know him, would return to him,
Her terrible familiar, dark and cool,
For whom she'd waited like a mortal bride,
Weakly, bravely, his queen of solitude.

The moon cried out unheard, its alien tongue
As distant and unmeaning as the steep
Abstraction of the ocean, a little cry.

What had she found? He saw himself go down
In search of her, pale and ridiculous,
And shivering beyond that golden road.
And he was begging in a puny voice
For death to yield his wife back up to him.

Where flesh fails, a white idea remains,
Regal and bloodthirsty in the shade.
It is his heart she holds, cold, in her hands.
Her face is turned. She will not speak to him.
Could that be her, averted, his poor girl,
A covert angel shrinking from his gaze?
She runs upon his heels in the loud murk
Of empty water, where he leads her back
From an immortal and demented hope.
It is not her. It never could be her.
The woman is a statue. Then himself,
Though strange to him. Then sickens into ash,
Mistress of misgiving, a mortal dream:
Who does not love a dying thing loves death.

He caught his breath. How hard it was, how strange!
He sat down on the sand and pitied her.

Rich Blind Minotaur
Led by a Girl

His elegance is but extenuation,
A makeshift courtesy to put from mind
That lethal elegance that mortifies,
Enslaves, and gives him bravery and force.
Despairing in his labyrinth he eats
The still-hot flesh of newly-murdered men;
Asleep, he slips between the sharpened horns
With other acrobats, no more a bull.

Her innocence was never ignorance.
Love takes us as we are, and at our worst
Loves us the better as our worst is ours.
She knows what maddens us is what we ought
To be and never are. She also knows
How little what we are is what we are.

Winter: Hunters in Snow

(from the Brueghel painting)

Before the baking-houses, the women
Stamp the snow from their feet.
Children fight on the frozen pond,
And at the edge of town, the drunkards
Warm their hands by the tavern fire.
But we pass through the trees
As if they were night's own ribs.

We have found only our own tracks:
The snares all sprung, with nothing in them,
No deer beyond the slanting
Shadows of the trees,
Not even a hare, shuddering in the snow
Beneath a thorn, wrapped in rings of wind.

We are like three strangers. Our boots
Are wet through, and instead of hares
We bring our cold hands.
The dark falls out of the trees.
A newborn child wails on an outlying farm.

In the Subway

Even with the crowd behind her straining
To climb out of the roaring dark and smoke
And her afraid of "acting like a fool"
He will step on before and take her hand
So she won't see he sees her hesitate
And carefully adopt a casual stance.
Then up they go, into the clear of noon
And April, dogwoods spreading ivory hands
And oaks resuming green and golden ease.
She makes a joke about Eurydice
But blames herself for what he loves her for,
How she might shy before a moving stair,
Yet lead them both, without a second's doubt,
Into the brave gay recklessness of love.

After the Thunderstorm

Again the crickets riot in the aloe-bush,
And the wide arroyo overflows.
Again, from under the acacia,
The lizards run like shadows on the sand.

You wake confused, but will not
Be deceived. For three days,
You tell yourself, the desert
Will be deranged; the gaudy sun
Will condense itself in flowers
Which throw their scents to every wind;
The cactuses will swell their ribs
Like men breathing deep;
And instead of sand, the air will blow with bees
But in three days, the shadow of rain
Will erase itself from the ground.

Fine. But at noon, alone,
You yourself will drink
The water standing in the pool,
And eat the banquets spread
By other hands, and stand
Atop a rock to view
The wide waste at its carnival.

It is not to be deceived, you will say,
But to enter into the deceits
With a full heart, and with open hands;
To lay your contradictions to one side,
And sing your three days' song
As if it were enough for life.

PUEBLO FAIRGROUNDS

The Zeppelin Watchers

(New Haven, 1918)

At first we saw in every cloud
The coming Huns, and when the light
Came to us from the yet unrisen moon
We ran to stations to fend off
A German fleet. Now we watch
The railyards rust, and play
Card games which never end.
Every day we practice aiming the big guns.
They crouch like insects basking in the sun.
In front of us, where the wind
Comes rushing up the cliff
The sparrow-hawks are circling
Like a squadron gone to sleep.
Sometimes, for lack of Zeppelins,
We shoot at them. Other times
We watch the ships come gliding past the bar,
Or feel the seasons pass us
Like the movement of a hand.
All day long we hear them living far below,
And every night the crickets
Scratch their names upon the air,
And the trees make sounds like breaking waves,
And the rivers at our feet lose themselves in reeds.
We could be idle gods
Sprawled awash in our own thoughts.

In the afternoon we send a runner down the rock
To say that we have nothing to report
And that the coast is clear.

Robert Falcon Scott
Enters Paradise

Then we heard our own breathing
And knew that the wind had dropped.
The sun descended like a bird of prey
And beat the sight from our eyes.
We stood astonished in the snow.

To the east, I saw mountains
Not on our map. Atop a pressure ridge
A mile away, I saw a man on foot
Crossing towards the range. The others
Shouted and waved their arms
But I sat down upon the sledge
And knew the length of time
We would remain upon the ice.

The Plague-Maiden

I was born on the shore
Of an Eastern sea
Where Turk and Christian
Bent to me.

And over the water,
In every land,
In every village,
Wherever they stand

They lay down their arms
And fall into peace.
Wherever I wander
Wanderings cease.

I gather the waste
And calm the complaint.
The criminal's cry
And the sigh of the saint

Are all of them music.
Will you come with me?
Or shall I come seeking
Where you chance to be:

By your hearth with your children,
In your bed by your bride,
Shall I climb in your window
And sit by your side?

Andrew Ramsay at the Somme

Only that which is the case is mine.
Of the rest, its sophistry, illusion,
And bloody beauty, I can tell you nothing,
Save that some men die for it when others
Tell them to. They do not show them facts,
Show them, say, the tense and garish light
Where every day we wait, or this hand
Which lately I have used for killing men.

What we cannot speak about we pass
In silence. It gestures to us from the dark,
Its purple robes shifting in rich menace
As it directs the birds to speak, the kings
To dance, and tells the secret history
We shall not understand until too late.

Plains of Peace

I have seen fools resist Providence before, and
I have seen their destruction, as will come upon
these again, utter destruction and contempt.
                    Woodrow Wilson, 1923

I. PHOTOGRAPH OF WILSON AT OPENING DAY, 1916

Behind him, the flicker of pennants, the April sun;
Around him his aides, betrayer and betrayed
Still mastered in the peace that he had bought;
At his side his wife, repressing a laugh,
Proud without the bitterness of pride.
His arm is crooked in mid-throw, awkward
But assured: the ball will drop, the game
Will run to rule, the winner and loser glad
To spend their summer in a dream of play.

It was not innocence: for two years
We had watched the endless slaughter overseas
And wrung our hands, although our hands were clean.
We sent them terms to solve their savagery,
As if reason were a reason, and we ourselves
Were more than men, our flesh drained of the hot
Unerring grievance of mortality.

These are the children that have fathered us,
Though we are not their sons, their heirs, their kin.

Shall we condescend to pity them,
Learned as we are in the wisdom of wrong?
Their errors seem like courage to us now.
We envy them the lives they threw away;
We envy them the hopes their hearts disproved;
But most of all, we envy him, his faith
That history had rules, that when the world
Careered into his grasp, a shuddering ball,
It would not come to pieces in his hands.

II. They Sing *Die Winterreise*
after the Armistice

Looking up at him, she waits for his nod.
Her fingers on the keys, the gathered sound
Like a drop about to fall, but not falling—
Something is happening. Why doesn't he nod?
The light quivers gold in the dense air
And her impatience wakens into fear.
This light is from Vermeer, come back to us
To hurt us with its beauty and reproach;
When last we sang these songs we were at peace.
Will we sing again, or will the light
Break and flare at stand-to till night falls?
We will be ghosts, who give ourselves to ghosts;
Yet let us have our light, and let him sing:
We love our errors or we lose our lives.
He will nod, and I will touch the chords
Softly, like the stirring of a wish
That the violence of love should be again
A form of innocence, and we again
Deceived, and rich in our deceits, as if
This song could be itself once more, and we
Could sing it as we did, just as we did.

III. Grayson on the Plains of Peace
(September 25, 1919)

In Donner Pass, as we strained up the grade
Through blazing trees, pressing tight our sleeves
Against our mouths to sift the panic-tainted
Air, the flames teasing the paint from the cars,
The branches beating on the glass like hands,
He dreamed the dead came laughing back from France,
Raising their stained palms, bemused in the mobs,
Winking when he spoke to them of peace.
At Reno, Salt Lake, Denver, the sky a big
Glass bell, the sun, breaking loose,
Stole the air from his lungs, till every word
Tripped and whirled in the sharp stink of fire,
And the weary, puzzled crowds, not wanting peace,
But just their boys again, stood there ashamed.
And when at Pueblo, that afternoon, he stopped,
And wept, and prophesied, and stopped again,
The papers called it "Wilson's Last Mad Act."
I pulled us to a siding out of town
And we went walking in the mild air
As the sun relented, and our shadows tossed
On the bright grass after us, and for an hour,
While the train lay still behind us, a dumb god

In his black brooding, knowing we would be his,
I almost thought we would have peace again,
As if we could remember it, and time
Would scour the confusion from our minds.

"It will be easier from here," he said.
Yes, I thought, easier to take the loss.
Then I sat down, the better to hold my tongue,
And wondered if in hell I'd still be pleading,
Threatening, bargaining, "For God's sake, give it up.
You know it's useless, and you're sick of it,"
Or whether hell will be a plain of peace,
Our burdens loosened there, our shame outlived,
An infinite extension of that hour.

And all at once, I saw him on a bridge,
Smiling at his error and his rage
As though we couldn't hurt him any more.
He waited there for me, on sun-raked steel
So bright it hurt my eyes. The little river
Laughed in its rapid dark, restored its secrets
Unexplained, unsoftened, all to him,
And the sky went sliding on like a sheet of glass,
As if no suffering were waste, no loss
An accident, and death a dream misplaced.
Beyond, a car was lifting up a plume
That twined and turned, glittering with dust,

And streamed across the cool and wind-washed grass.
He was not one of us. I stood there staring,
Full of my wish and half afraid of it.
Then a jet snorted, swirling from the wheels.
The firebox door chunked open; the engine tensed,
Steam up full, its motion just withheld.
He turned and smiled at me, and picked his way
In the late light, ready now at last.

But on the train, I could not speak to him.
I stood in the vestibule and watched the tracks
Converging far behind us, how the land
Rushed and shrank together as we rolled.
The distant mountains flared, and in the blaze
The scavengers were gliding, following.

IV. SENATOR FALL'S REPORT

(December 4, 1919)

Yes, Mr. Lodge, they didn't keep me from him;
Weren't at all surprised. They had him dressed,
Even shaved. They'd propped him at his desk.
His wife sat out of earshot, glaring at us
As if I were the sick one. I let her play
By her own rules: her court, her handicap.
It was easy to be fair, considering.
He raised an arm to put it on the desk,
Thumb and fingers pinching at the cuff
The way you pick a cat up by the neck,
Meanwhile looking calmly at me, daring me
To see it. "Well?" he said, his voice quite clear
And just a trifle loud. I went on down
The whole list: Mexico, the reparations . . .
He looked out the window as I spoke,
Waiting, bored, for me to muff my lines,
As if he'd prompt me only when I'd paused
Just long enough to show that I was lost.
When I rose to go, he smiled at me,
"Does that satisfy you, Mr. Fall?"
I was ashamed. I said I wished him well.
Then his wife led me out like a captive bear.
Nothing there for us. Still, he won't bend
On the Reservations. We'll get him there, I guess.

V. THE BRICK ARCH

Sure the crowds were big, and the show was something:
People shouting my name, flags all snapping,
Thrills of brass, soldiers presenting arms,
Veterans wheeled up front so they could see
(Harding would say this later, to his friends),
But I was uneasy, and took no pleasure in it
—Or I shouldn't have—sitting there with him.
"My God, the man's a wreck," I heard them say
As we went by. I was afraid he'd hear,
But he just sat as if he were alone.
I'm still not sure he knew just where he was,
And if he didn't, then it was a mercy.

What could I do? I sat there shivering.
"I hope my dogs won't get the staff upset,"
I said at last, and he just looked at me.
Well, I thought, at least I don't keep elephants.

A few blocks from the Capitol, I saw
That tears were dribbling down his jaw. How
Do you tell a President to wipe his face?
Just as we stopped, he did the job himself,
And I was glad I hadn't said a thing.

Since then, I've had this dream again and again
(He would say this to his wife, alone in the dark)
That I sat with the angel of judgment in a slow car
—But it was that old man—and he looked for the saved
Among the crowds there, scornful and unflinching,
Weighing all our souls against his own,
And finding not one worthy, no, not one.

Sonnets for Mary of Nazareth

I

Our gods resemble us only in rage,
Where we are undissembled, undisclosed,
A cryptic self we'd never recognize,
Not what we are, not what we'd ever be,
But what escapes us, makes us real.
To find a god, we must break all things else,
Lest we be left with what he's like, not him.
In angry certitude, baffled gracefully,
We seek more cunning ways to disavow
What thrilled us once, when it could still be strange,
What stung us into truth with daring cruelty.
We want an idol made of restlessness.
That is the discontent the flesh would have
Hung over with a three days drunk of death.

II

Homer's gods, bored with endless life,
Loved mortals, whose fragile bodies puzzled them.
How suddenly they came apart! How little
One discovers after all from them.
There is some secret in them they don't know,
That shadows them in love, then intimates
Some deeper source, which sought for, vanishes.
One looks abashed into a glassy eye.

Achilles sought to kill his way to fame,
Immortal through excess, a man made god.
Wide-eyed, happy in the clash of shields,
It did not matter to him what he was.
Nor did he matter, till he saw in tears
Priam with his duty-smitten son.

III

Because he was so plain a god, so calm,
Riding at her heart like any child,
A stirring and attentive passenger
Wakeful in her wordless rush of breath,
She would have been amused, not terrified.
What did he have in mind? she thought at nights
While patient Joseph snored and shepherds woke.
It came to her at last: he didn't know;
He himself would catch it up from her.
What could he want, except to want like her?
To know what weakness is, and casualty,
How being done to teaches her to be,
How losing love enables her to learn
To make of fear her honor and of death her gift.

Nocturne

Looking behind me, as I closed the door,
I saw, in their quiet rows, unblinking,
The wakeful eyes of the oscilloscopes,
How they regarded me, severe and calm,
And made me too aware of drawing breath.
Outside I did not see a soul, not one.
The branches moved and moved in endless trouble,
Shaking down their darkness over me,
Until at last, I saw another man,
The night disc-jockey, dancing all alone
Behind his window, in a yellow room.
I watched there half a minute as he turned
To unheard music in an ecstasy
I was no part of, and would not understand;
But I was glad of heart, and overhead
I saw an airplane crossing, west to east.

St. Francis and the Wolf

I

Saved at last, not at the last of me,
I knelt two-legged, made of guttural air
A little yelp to sound like human prayer.
The saints were cautious, understandably.

I took the cup, and managed not to drool,
But dreamed the wine was blood, as I'd been taught,
And vainly curbed the vain bent of my thought.
I knew myself an angel, felt a fool.

Could God have erred in making teeth and maw?
Then for his glory I will bite the lamb
Whose terror he transmogrifies to awe
That I may do his service as I am,

Till as I am I leap the mortal gulf
To rage in heaven, a perfected wolf.

II

Sometimes, when I am rapt past God in prayer
God grants me sight of what I kneel before
And there I am, bolt-wielding, brawny-voiced,
Having it all my way, uneasy still.
God mocks me with me, and I with him
Unwittingly have done the same. Sometimes
I worship force, and sometimes me, until
Enraged and sick, I would forget it all

Except what sickens me with self and force.
I've never worshipped anything but wrong;
Without belief I'll worship nothing else.
I am, like you, a wolf, but you, like me
Might not be only wolf, though what you are
God only knows, who blessed with bafflement.

Trucks on a Hill in Winter

Each truck, as it passes you, breaks off its cry,
Rumbles lower, renews the thick complaint.
The breathless sentry lamps bend over them
In thin helmets, arrayed in splinters,
Streaming their blue chill down steadily.
They dry the grass with their strict attention.

But on the ridge beyond, the ranks of towers flash,
Their glittering contrails streaking from the ground.
What does it matter that the night is cold,
You say, and past you, on the grade,
The shifting engines raise their round: long haul
Up the long haul up the long
Haul up the hill.

Thomaston Dam

Grudgingly becomes a monument,
A rubble bow between the hills. The tracks
Stretch from the cut to muscle down the arc,
Their mica-glitter urgent in the blaze
As the dumb intent that laid the terminal
Moraine. The lake is down; again the stream
Moves at leisure through the junk-flecked grass,
Again the gray trees wash themselves with red.

They move in calmly. If they don't forgive,
Neither do they laugh. Beyond, the water
Bubbles in the gorge, and over the trees
The spires of town crop up, and the brick
Chimney of the factory where, for years,
They have built clocks although marooned in age.

Notes

"The Funeral Day": Tobacco in Connecticut is grown in the shade of large cheesecloth shrouds.

"From the Diary of Willard Gibbs": Josiah Willard Gibbs, after a lifetime of publishing important research in obscure journals, became famous at the end of his life for his theories about Thermodynamics and the Entropy Law, and for creating the theoretical framework for Statistical Mechanics. Evariste Galois, unable to publish the papers which now form the basis for Group Theory, sent his proofs to Carl Friedrich Gauss the evening before he was killed in a duel.

"His Kind-Hearted Woman": Robert Johnson, the blues singer, was reputed to have learned to play from the devil. Although there are many theories about his mysterious early death, he is usually said to have been poisoned by a jealous lover.

"Leonce Pontellier": The characters of this poem are drawn from Kate Chopin's *The Awakening*. The poem is set just after Edna Pontellier's suicide, which closes the novel.

"The Zeppelin Watchers": All through the First World War fifty soldiers manned an anti-Zeppelin gun battery atop East Rock in New Haven, Connecticut. The foundation of the battery can still be seen.

"Andrew Ramsay at the Somme": Andrew Ramsay is a character from Virginia Woolf's *To the Lighthouse*. I have made him, like his father, a philosopher, putting in his mouth some of the more famous beliefs of the logical positivists. Woolf does not say in what battle Andrew was killed. For my description of those things Andrew, following Wittgenstein, says we cannot talk about, I have turned to another of Woolf's war casualties, Septimus Warren Smith of *Mrs. Dalloway*.

"Plains of Peace": The epigraph is Wilson's last public utterance, to a group of veterans who came to his door asking for a speech on Armistice Day, 1923. During the spring of 1916 Wilson was engaged in fruitless attempts to negotiate an end to the First World War, attempts partly undermined by his own Secretary of State, whom Wilson himself later betrayed in his madness. Admiral Grayson was Wilson's, and later Harding's, personal physician. I have loosely followed the account of the hours between Wilson's Pueblo speech and his stroke given in Gene Smith's *When the Cheering Stopped*. Senator Albert Fall, later the chief criminal in the Teapot Dome affair, was dispatched by Senator Henry Cabot Lodge, Wilson's principal antagonist, to discuss with Wilson what he planned to do about the seizure of the American Consulate in Veracruz by Mexican revolutionaries. In fact Fall's aim was to discover whether the President was in his right mind. Wilson made a worse fool of him than I have allowed him to do in the poem.

77

LIBRARY OF CONGRESS

Library of Congress Cataloging-in-Publication Data

Burt, John, 1955-
The way down / by John Burt.

p. cm. — (Princeton series of contemporary poets)
ISBN 0-691-06727-9 (alk. paper) ISBN 0-691-01443-4
(pbk.)
I. Title. II. Series.
PS3552.U767W39 1988   87-29619
811'.54—dc19